Serenading the
DAWN

Poetry and musings

SHIROMA PERERA-NATHAN

Published in Australia by Sid Harta Publishers Pty Ltd,
ABN: 46 119 415 842
23 Stirling Crescent, Glen Waverley, Victoria 3150 Australia
Telephone: +61 3 9560 9920, Facsimile: +61 3 9545 1742
E-mail: author@sidharta.com.au

First published in Australia 2019
This edition published 2019
Copyright © Shiroma Perera-Nathan 2019
Cover design, typesetting: WorkingType (www.workingtype.com.au)

The right of Shiroma Perera-Nathan to be identified as the Author of the Work has been asserted in accordance with the Copyright, Designs and Patents Act 1988.

This book is a work of fiction. Any similarities to that of people living or dead are purely coincidental.

The Author of this book accepts all responsibility for the contents and absolves any other person or persons involved in its production from any responsibility or liability where the contents are concerned.

All rights reserved. No part of this publication may be reproduced, stored in a retrieval system, or transmitted, in any form or by any means without the prior written permission of the publisher, nor be otherwise circulated in any form of binding or cover other than that in which it is published and without a similar condition being imposed on the subsequent purchaser.

Shiroma Perera-Nathan
Serenading the Dawn: Poetry And Musings
ISBN: 978-1-925230-70-3
pp128

Also by Shiroma Perera-Nathan
Gemini's Reflection

Gemini's
REFLECTION

Poetry By
Shiroma Perera-Nathan & Sasheeka Costa

Shiroma Perera-Nathan was born in Sri Lanka. When she was five, her family migrated to New Zealand and later as an adult she moved to Australia, where she currently resides. Shiroma co-manages cafe and coffee roasting business, CoffeeHead, with her chef husband, Ashanth, and business partner, Bill, in between writing, which serves as her creative outlet. She is the co-author of *Gemini's Reflection*, her first anthology of poetry and is at present researching for her planned third book on The Old Vic Tour of Australia and New Zealand in 1948, headed by Sir Laurence Olivier and Vivien Leigh. Shiroma lives in Melbourne with her husband, children, Sean and Christina, and a very spoiled Siamese cat, Lady Olivier.

Disclaimer

This is a book of childhood memories, nostalgia, love and inspirations. The author's poetry is hers and inspired by her life experiences and imagination. Any similarity to anyone else's imagination, work and life is coincidence only. Every effort has been made to give credit and due notation where direct quotes have been used or inspiration sought from non-fictional sources. With the exception of deceased public figures, whose lives have been nothing but inspiring, and family members living, whose permission has been obtained, any other resemblance to persons living or dead is purely coincidental. The author is a romantic poetess, wishing for a time machine, not a fighter.

Dedication

Vivien Leigh

You are the inspirer of my words,
possessor of my heart,
introducer to film and theatre,
expander of my knowledge,
influencer of my travels,
and forever the serenader of dawn.

Acknowledgements

Eternal thanks and gratitude to the following angels, for without you there would be no words.

Ashanth Nathan, my rock and life partner. Thank you for giving me the space and opportunity to do what I love.

Sean Patrick and Christina Scarlett, the reason for my life; the children that have come through me, not from me.

Leela Kumari, my grandmother, teacher of my first words.

My makers and life-givers, Stanley and Kanthi.

Grandfather, Richard; Great-Aunt, Anula Kumari; Aunts Malini, Janakee and Nita; Uncles Gamini, and Luxman; and maid, Kamala, who together formed my childhood world of wonder. You gave me the perfect first five years in Ceylon.

My brother, Sherman, who shared my first home five years after me.

Sasheeka Costa, my Gemini soul-sister.

Serge Mafioly, the ever-charming French gentleman and author of *Vivien Leigh, "D'air Et De Feu"* who encouraged me to start writing by starting a journal.

Peter Wilson, with the blue eyes; my Intermediate school teacher who appreciated my first verse titled *Seagull* many years ago – wherever you are.

Kerry B Collison, for whom all roads of Sid Harta Publishing are paved and leads.

Marie Pietersz, for her invaluable advice, help, direction and editing.

Virosh Perera, for his support and help from day one.

Luke Harris, for his designing talent, technical support, advice and confidence.

Peter Eerden, for making my favourite Notley even better.

And finally, but with all my sincerity and gratitude, to my friends in Vivien Leigh fandom, who have given me encouragement and supported my writing and because of whom Vivien's memory stays alive.

Special mention must go to:

Kendra Bean, my most revered friend, author of *Vivien Leigh, an Intimate Portrait* and web mistress of the most compressive online resource on Vivien Leigh and Laurence Olivier: *vivandlarry.com*. Thank you for your advice, help and friendship over the years.

Alejandro Franks, Vice Chair of Vivien Leigh Circle, my illustrator, for his artistic talent, support and commitment to the Vivien Leigh Circle.

Carol Anderson, who travelled far for my first book and christened the Vivien Leigh decanter and wine glasses with me.

Esperanza Alcastle, for her friendship and who, all the way from Spain, understands my inner world.

Greta Ritchie, from Nebraska for her appreciation and confidence in my work.

Rebecca Pool Gilbert, for her online friendship and to whom I am the "Clair de Lune" gal.

Christina Bystrom, who flew to New York just to say, 'Hello' and to whom I signed my first book.

Contents

Introduction 1

Ceylon 5

Sorrow 25

Notley 41

Vivien 51

Children 71

Love 85

Introduction

"The fields lay sleeping whitely—
Now and then a little rustle thro' the corn
Only our footsteps shattered the stillness
And then we saw the magic of the dawn—
And we loved — Then
We thanked God for
the enchantment of the mountains."

Vivien Leigh, June 11, 1931*

I was born in the picturesque hill country town of Kandy, Sri Lanka. Surrounded by mountains that house many tea estates and rain forests, its beautiful lake takes centre-stage. Kandy also houses the only surviving relic of Lord Buddha – the sacred tooth, which is kept at the Sri Dalada Maligawa (The Temple of the Sacred Tooth Relic).

Like its name suggests, Kandy and its surrounding tea estates provided the perfect backdrop for a child to develop a good imagination – tranquil, beautiful, and straight from the pages of a Kipling poem.

Growing up, I was left to my own devices, being the youngest

---

* *Vivien Leigh's personal poetry in part, quoted from Auction Item 855 by RR Auction. Handwritten book of poetry kept by Leigh during the late 1920s and early 1930s containing 170 pages in her hand, mostly comprising transcriptions of works by famous writers, as well as several original compositions.* www.rrauction.com

by many years within an extended family scenario. My maternal grandfather was an estate superintendent, so we lived mostly on tea plantations.

I'd spend hours walking and imagining things. My favourite pastime was to take a stick to draw on the dirt and tell stories to myself. Scribbling in the dirt occupied many hours. Life is simple as a child when you live in a world of peace, beauty and love – for surely, this is how I remember those formative years.

Over the years growing up, I've always preferred to write when I've had the time, felt inspired, or wanted to communicate my feelings; real pens and paper, typewriters and computers taking the place of the stick and dirt.

The words in this collection have been inspired by this childhood in Sri Lanka, my loves, my children, life experiences, heartbreaks, vulnerabilities, dreams, friendships and, of course, Vivien.

My poetry has been dedicated to Vivien Leigh, English film and stage actress, who has without doubt been my biggest inspiration. Not only has the title been inspired by a piece that she wrote in a notebook, but many of my own words have been either inspired by her life or are about her, accounting for a whole section dedicated to her. The poetry, although inspired by her, is, I believe, timeless and I hope will echo your own life experiences. Love, after all, is a universal theme.

They say there is a story inside all of us; a story worth telling. These are my stories.

As ever
Yours
Shiroma

These Musings

These musings
Reflecting windows of my soul,
Stained glass by tears of longing.
These musings
Dancing like childhood footsteps on rain-washed tiles,
Silver edged from longings for nostalgia.
These musings
Leaving marks slowly disappearing,
Today they bathe in the moon's seraphic glaze.
These musings
Screaming in silence of love undeclared,
Ballads to love lost and gained.
These musings
Singing her words, her life, her love, her loss,
Limericks to her lyrebird lore.
These musings
Erasing the unbearable lightness of her being.
They started as scribbles on Ceylon's* red soil.
These musings
Swaddling dreams yet to bloom,
Truth confessed ... serenading the dawn!

---

* *Sri Lanka was formerly called Ceylon whilst under British colonial rule. In this book it will be referred to as Ceylon for lyrical and nostalgic purposes.*

CEYLON

Mt Lavinia sea shore and hotel

Mt Lavinia sea shore as envisioned during the early 1900s. In the foreground on the cliff stands Mt Lavinia Hotel, named after Lovinia Aponsuwa, a local Sinhalese/Portuguese dancer, renowned for her beauty. The Victorian mansion, which stands on the bluff overlooking the beautiful Indian Ocean, was built by British Ceylon's second Governor, Sir Thomas Maitland. It was the setting of their illicit love affair. He built it

with a secret tunnel leading directly to Lovinia's humble hut in a nearby fishing village. Love between an English nobleman and a low-caste local girl was unacceptable and risky during those times. It had to be kept a secret. It is said that for seven years, Lovinia made her way to her lover's mansion via the tunnel and stayed only till dawn.

The Eden of the Sea

"Ceylon! Ceylon! 'tis nought to me
How thou wert known or named of old,
As Ophir, or Taprobane,
By Hebrew king, or Grecian **bold:** *-*
To me, thy spicy-wooded vales,
Thy dusky sons, and jewels bright,
But image forth the far-famed tales-
But seem a new Arabian Night."

Mary Jane Jewsbury[*]

---

[*] Mary Jane Jewsbury was an English writer, poet and literary reviewer. In 1832, after marrying Rev William K Fletcher, one of the chaplains of the East India Company, she went with him to India. They spent the Christmas week of 1832 on the shores of Port Louise. Quote of 8th verse from The Eden of the Sea, Oceanides, published 1833.

My Ceylon

She, the land of the mighty Lion's roar,
A loving Grandmother's comfort,
The mystical adventure cove of Sinbad,
My Ceylon!

She, the imposing rock fortress of Sigiriya,
The never known love of a lost sister,
The majesty of Buddha's sacred Bo Tree,
My Ceylon!

She, the Serendipity of past lore,
Memories of the perfect childhood,
The nostalgic teardrop pearl of India,
My Ceylon!

She, the turbulent scene of Elephant Walk,
Red earth soil that spoke the first story,
The second jewel in the Imperial Crown,
My Ceylon!

She, the banished retreat of Prince Vijaya,
Lush rainforests, walked in wonder,
The green leaf world-renowned,
My Ceylon!

She, the noble tangerine robe of monks,
Rolling tea plains, we ran through,
The exalted heiress of Asian oceans,
My Ceylon!

She, the aromatic garden of cinnamon,
Friendship of our loyal maids,
The frescoes dancing at the citadel,
My Ceylon!

She, the welcoming hands of Ayubowan,*
Queenly blue sapphire on a wedded finger,
The wisdom of the nine skies bridge,
My Ceylon!

She, the mystery of the mist settling,
Melting ice cream, tasted at Perahera,†
The worthy custodian of Buddha's relic,
My Ceylon!

She, the magnificence of a peacock's tail,
The grace of the fishermen's flying net,
The devoted pilgrim ascending Adam's Peak,
My Ceylon!

She is Ceylon, **my** Ceylon!

---

*   Ayubowan – *with two hands joined together in a prayer-like manner, salutation, wishing the recipient a long life, typically a greeting or goodbye.*

†   Perahera – *Kandy's oldest and grandest Buddhist festival featuring procession of decorated elephants.*

Galagedera

Last night I dreamt of Galagedera,*
Red earth soil beneath my feet.

The black-stoned wall holds the bungalow high,
Like my mind of childhood memories.

Dusty scribbles on the ground,
Disappear in humid slow-motioned gust.

The magenta bougainvillea in full bloom,
Trying to embrace me in a loving trance.

The path canopied with capturing trees,
Jasmine entangled in the mist.

Large windows reflect the moon's celestial web,
And there, through one,
Grandma's voice calls me ... Sudu.†

---

* Galagedera – (house of stone), village in Central Province of Sri Lanka.
† Sudu – term of endearment, meaning "white".

Kandy Town

Cacophony of tuk tuks* outside,
Crowds lining the sacred temple,
Bestowed in white like a bride.

Lotus garlands of magenta profusion,
Offerings to part of He who resides,
Carpet fragrance, ancient floor's illusion.

Past the iconic clock tower,
Through a sea of red buses,
Stroll the lakeside, gated like a flower.

The Queen's,† a relic of the Empire,
Trinity‡ schoolboys playing cricket
On a field of dreams, with an umpire.

Then at last, the Kandy Bake House,
Pastel mini ribbon cake, fragrant tea,
Little girl might've past future spouse!

---

*   *Tuk tuk – auto rickshaw.*
†   *The Queen's Hotel – iconic colonial hotel from the British Empire.*
‡   *Author's husband, Ashanth Nathan, is a former student of Trinity College.*

Matale Winds

Down there on the distant path,
Grandpa's swaggering home;
Hill myna flutters in his bird bath,
Prayers float from temple dome.

Under the shade of the mango tree,
Little feet stomp impatiently;
Gifts he brings fills her childish glee,
Kamala, servant girl, walks hastily
Bringing water pots on her hips;
Quick, before darkness falls.
Light the oil wick lamps before it drips,
Gobble down Grandma's rice balls.

Incense-lit flowers to Vishnu,[*]
Household gathers around the radio,
Matale[†] winds whisper through bamboo.

---

[*] *Vishnu – one of the three principle deities in Hinduism.*
[†] *Matale – town in Central Province in Sri Lanka.*

Leela Kumari

Nestled in her warm embrace,
Rain falling heavily outside
disturbing rolling plains of tea shrubs —
I am four again.

Broad forehead, black hair curled,
Slender eyebrows, thin aquiline nose,
Bow-like sweet lips that taught me my first words,
Talented hands that helped mine trace her writing.

When grandpa's laughter stopped one day,
I was growing up in Aotearoa;[*]
The flute played by the monk in the temple
… continued a melancholy tune.

The fragrance of the incense held in the bronze holders,
Floated through the bungalow;
When I went back to comfort her —
I was by then eighteen.

---

* Aotearoa – Maori name for New Zealand, meaning 'long white cloud'.

Apsaras

They float on billowy clouds, his nymphs,
High above the mortal plains;*
Cloaking in their sheltered alcove,
Adorned in coral clues, they dance
Serenading his heavenly theme;
For were they drawn to entice my love,
These winsome deer-eyed ones;
Resplendent ladies, heaven appears,
Thereafter death does not perturb.

---

* *The rock fortress of Sigiriya was the castle of King Kashyapa (circa 477–495 CE). An engineering marvel, it covered three acres of pleasure gardens, palaces and temples. The western wall was decorated with hundreds of colourful frescoes, of which only eighteen survive today – they are called the Apsaras: cloud damsels and lightening princesses. Sigiriya is a UNESCO listed World Heritage Site.*

Worshipping Hour

Oh! evening hour of worship approach,
Let that mystical memory encroach.

The ripple of her ivory sari moves,
Sunset caresses the Dagoba* divine,
Poson† full moon appears to love
Impending darkness, reflects her shine.

Oh! evening hour of worship approach,
Feel again my childhood encroach.

Smoldering incense perfumes the night,
Fragile lotus blossoms she carries,
Ignite the oil lamps, bringing light,
Whispering venerations, she tarries.

Oh! evening hour of worship approach,
Heavenly heart of Buddhism encroach.

---

* Dagoba – a hemispherical shrine that houses sacred relics.
† Poson full moon – Poya day is a day in June when Buddhists celebrate the arrival of Buddhism to Ceylon in 3rd Century BC.

Devoted pilgrim, empty mortal dream
Like lamps, eliminating darkness,
Dispel ignorance, to bring inward beam
To walk in truth and footstep's softness.

Grandmother's Song

As morning makes her appearance,
Grandmother's song comes to me
Softly, softly,
Like Areca nut palms that sway
Caressing the edge of the paddy field.

Taking me back through the vista of years,
Till I can clearly hear her melody,
Softly, softly,
Like the trill of a flute's rhythm
Drifting on the Mahaweli River.

Wistful tears take me back,
Her voice coming to carry me aboard,
Softly, softly,
Like the gentle Nuwara Eliya fog
Kissing trails through wavy hilltops.

I am home.

Rebirth

We seemed to have loved an eternity
As grandmother and grandchild;
You and I, playing the songs of every poet,
Like that time I was born in Ceylon.

Your soul will find mine
Again, and again,
In the next — be reborn in my womb,
Like that time I was born in Ceylon.

Then I can love you,
Teach and nurture you,
Give back to you what you gave me,
Like that time I was born in Ceylon.

Morning Dream

I woke this morning, remembering Ceylon,
The sound of rain gracing recollections;
Memories billowing through chiffon,
Softly washing over blurred visions,
Wishing to drift back into my dream;
Small feet walking through rubber plantations
Searching for my first love—
She was gone.

Poetess of Ceylon

Leela,* wherever your gentle spirit rests,
I hope you're proud of me.
Leela, I've learnt my life's passion,
I first saw it as you took my hands.
Leela, I wrote my first words with your grace,
I hope I didn't disappoint you.
Leela, you left me stranded in Ceylon's memory,
I've lived a million heartaches since.
Leela, from my unbearable sadness,
I started painting words of empathy.
Leela, I draw them with the tears I drip,
I present to you my poetry.
Leela, I hope you're proud of me.

---

* *Leela is the author's maternal grandmother, teacher of her first words.*

SORROW

Vivien Leigh in costume for The Happy Hypocrite*

---

*   *Sketch of rare photograph by Norman Parkinson of Vivien Leigh as Jenny Mere in Max Beerbohm's production of* The Happy Hypocrite, *1936.*

On Joy and Sorrow:

"When you are joyous, look deep into your heart and you shall find it is only that which has given you sorrow that is giving you joy.
When you are sorrowful look again in your heart, and you shall see that in truth you are weeping for that which has been your delight."

THE PROPHET*
Kahlil Gibran

---

* *The Prophet* is a book of 26 prose poetry fables by poet and writer, Kahlil Gibran. The prose is delivered as sermons by Almustafa, a wise man who has been living on the fictional island of Orphalese. As he is about to set sail back to his homeland, the people of the island ask him to share his wisdom on: love, family, work, sorrow, joy, marriage and death. He is the third best-selling poet of all time behind Shakespeare and Laozi. Since it was published in 1923, *The Prophet* has never been out of print. It has been translated into fifty languages and is constantly on best-seller lists. Kahlil's work has inspired not only song lyrics, but also political speeches. The excerpt is part of the prose fable, 'On Joy And Sorrow'.

Depth

She breathed when there was no air
To give to those she held dear.
She could've been someone,
But she didn't know how;
In an antipodal world that was suffocating,
She finds it hard to move and she's not visible—
Will this pass too?

And so, she slept even though the sun shone
And her children played;
Hoping to awake to the answer,
But her brown pools of desperation opened
To a wound deeper
And numbness took over.

Feelings were of no use,
For each attempt another failure;
Who said there was a rainbow at the end?
She only found an ocean that drowned her
And the mermaid who took her there.

Lost

Autumn leaves drop from trees and fly
Forgotten like our dreams;
Candles lit in silent prayer
Where once our wishes went;
The chest of treasures we dived for
Still buried deep unfound …

Hopes and visions from summers gone,
Frozen by winter's snow;
Laughter and joy from our field of dreams
Echoes in a lost horizon.

Goals and aspirations cry to fly
Like birds with broken wings;
Failure and heartache from unattained goals
Floating painfully down memory's enraptured river.

Broken

Pieces of me that you chiseled away
Take pride in your masterpiece of con artistry;
When did the awareness come, darling?
As Ella gave away her wisdom; that is when it dawned.

Hope was a long-gone illusion
Stolen by him with no regret;
How long did you stare at the ticking clock, darling?
Till he chipped the final piece with the knife of disillusionment; that is when it stopped ticking.

Fake facades take too much energy,
When he pushed me to wear the mask of disheartenment;
What made you discard the forced smile, darling?
Until it was still believed, still believed, she echoed; that is when I dropped it.

Took as much as I could carry,
Including heavy tears muffled by salty pride;
When did the floodgates open, darling?
As I lay in painful solitude by the edge of world's end; that is when it poured.

And when the ebony night swallowed the blood moon,
I packed the bags of yesterday with
Passion blooming ...
When did you decide to leave, darling?
As the twilight door opened into an awakening; that is when I rose.

Heartbreak

My heart was a blank sheet in my guarded diary
Until you came and carved your name across it—
Now it bleeds these words, in an attempt to heal.

Arrow Through the Heart

The radiance of the dawn
That sang your arrival, is grey and bitter;
The vermillion sun that appeared always
Now in hiding;
The nightingale that brought your notes
Pierced herself like a thorn bird
When your arrow killed the peacock that danced in my heart
for you.

Leaving

And there she floats into the world of crimson sunsets
Where anything is possible, and nothing is awry;

And she leaves behind landslides of tears,
Children yet to grow,

And she feels the burdens lifting
Though the one last glance is painful;

And she extends her hand to be pulled up to resting
They then embrace her – all those gone;

And hence they came ... her grandmother's sweet breath,
Vivling,* the child she never saw, friends lost and her
imagined love.

---

*   *Vivling – term of endearment Ernest Hartley used for his daughter, Vivien Leigh – short for Vivien Darling*

Darkness

Worthlessness washes ashore yet again,
Not calm but a thrashing,
Like a million arrows it pierces my existence,
Constant without rest.
I wonder where the meaning is,
Where a light is supposed to guide
Has been extinguished.
Here rolls in the first thoughts of
Darkness, as I descend.

Once and Now

Once, when I adored you and you lifted me to Everest,
Sunday's goodbye turned to Monday's hello.

Once, when you looked at me with lustful eyes,
I smiled back at you and we nearly touched.

Once, when you were so eager to teach,
I felt like I had wings and the world was amazing.

Once is now, when you walk past and I am invisible,
And I wish the breath you take inhaled me.

Once is now, when I hear you speak to another,
And I wish hearing you would make me deaf.

Once is now, when you don't acknowledge my existence,
And I wish to feel the wind that caresses your shirt.

Once is now, as I erase these words,
And I wish the will you imprinted disappears.

Regret

Remember that moonlit night
When we walked perilously close to the precipice—
That cliff called love—
We never quiet reached it;
But I considered it,
Then walked away.

Solitude

A hiding sun playing with a bleak day,
Carpeted by a chalcedony sea;
Salty air moistening my lips,
This moment's peace will belong only to me.

Crashing sea, foreboding an eerie emptiness,
Song of the wind welcomes a symphony for misty tidings
As she settles on the sea's face like a veil.

Solitude ...
Only one comes to mind in my solitude.

Last Hour

When death made his appearance,
She whispered softly caressing her last breath—
"Please, one more hour to tell him I love him. I have always loved him."

NOTLEY

Notley Abbey, an Augustinian abbey built in the 12th century, Buckinghamshire, England, was once the home of Laurence Olivier and Vivien Leigh. Olivier said that of all the houses he had lived in, Notley was his favourite. There, he had an affair with the past and the abbey mesmerised him. Tarquin Olivier, Olivier's son from his first marriage to Jill Esmond, re-quoted a description he provided to Vivien Leigh's biographer, Anne Edwards, in his book, My Father, Laurence Olivier, "In a great valley it lay- the heart of leafy Buckinghamshire, the river Thame meandering in weedy shallows through the elm woods, the willowed fields. The place where Henry V once stayed, breathed heraldry. In the attic were priceless frescoes of the emblem of Notley embracing the hazel nut and the

lover's knot." pg. 137. The years at Notley were some of the best in the Olivier/ Leigh marriage. Tarquin also remembered that he had never seen a man and woman in love, and at Notley, their passion, and depth of experiences shared was reborn, pg. 142. Vivien said that it was the only home she had ever known.

The Abbey today is owned by Bijou Wedding Venues and is an award-winning wedding venue. The author had the privilege of spending a night there when she attended a wedding in July 2016. The verse following was inspired by her time there and the years Leigh and Olivier called it home.

Notley of yesteryear – you do remember 'that house', my dear!
Come, take my hand, and through Larry's canopied lime walk
You and I meander
Over the bridge, around the bend and hold our breath
As the past transposes present.
See, we are enraptured at her appearance.
Yes! We have stepped through the mirror, you and I
Together as promised so long ago …

Notley of yesteryear – you're still so enchanting, my dear!
Butterflies over lavender flutter,
Blood roses stand stark against pillars;
We feel the lover's knot tightening our hearts
And like those before us, we've fallen under that spell.

Notley of yesteryear – you're still mesmerising, my dear!
Her image that we've only imagined,
Has suddenly assumed reality;
And as the July sun baths her in golden splendour,
She awaits her guests in former glory.

Notley of yesteryear – you're still inspiring passion, my dear!
Lovers make vows and declare eternal unity,
Friends and family gather under falling petals
And you and I bask in sublimity;
Then she'll come alive with lights ablaze and harmonies played.

Notley of yesteryear – you exist in a fairy tale, my dear!
The swirling Thames that meanders through her, gurgling at twilight,
Its lily pads making perfect floats, above the war of weeds;
And at the witching hour, dragonflies transform to forest nymphs
As we walk bare-footed on her moss-green veil, the moon watches.

Notley of yesteryear – you're still captivating in our rest, my dear!
As we nestle in between warm sheets, at ease in our friendship,
Amorous past tales echo through doors,
And England's sweet summer scent blows
Through her ancient arched windows like a whispered lullaby.

Notley of yesteryear – you're still wondrous to observe, my dear!
See the morning dew sparkling on her dress, as we sit in our peace
And when the doves alight beyond yonder cove,
They bring a morning song,
With nature as backing symphony.

Notley of yesteryear – still a paradox, my dear!
She delights and make us smile;
Then, next in a moment of contemplation makes us cry.
Hamlet has left taking Sabina, the glasshouse shattered
And chimneys no longer tell their stories.

Notley of yesteryear – you're still the one we return to, my dear!
Even though no fragranced potpourri in her corridors,
Nor walls lined with treasured collections
And those that walked through Vivien's folly are long gone;
The thousand white roses she loved vanished,
Still, she enchanted like no other.

Now take my hand again, let's skip through Larry's
lime walk like children,
No, don't look back ... there is no need;
Step again through the mirror, returning reality.
Notley of yesteryear – it's not goodbye but *jusqu'au revoir*,
my sweetest, dearest darling.

VIVIEN

Serenading the Dawn

O Lyric Love

"O Lyric Love, half-angel and half-bird
And all a wonder and a wild desire—
Boldest of hearts that ever braved the sun."

The Ring and the Book
ROBERT BROWNING

Robert Browning was an English poet and playwright. The Ring and the Book is a long narrative poem, published in 12 books from 1868 to 1869. "O Lyric Love" is the concluding passage in Book 1 where he describes his late wife who had been his muse. Alan Dent, author of Vivien Leigh, A Bouquet, quoted these lines to Vivien, in a conversation and she was quick to say, 'Why do you never pin upon me such a beautiful brooch of a quotation when you write?' pg. 11. He writes that he pinned it there for her to wear, but alas too late as she had passed when he wrote the book. Being the author's muse as well, it is herewith pinned too.

Darjeeling's* Child

An Indian sunset welcomed a stunning child,
Perfect symphony of looks compiled!

A garden of azaleas and lilies bloomed,
For a life that would be forever perfumed!

Himalayan majesty glistened blue,
The prettiest guy to be born ... true!

Great destiny written on her palm,
So much life, to be never calm!

To scale the impossible heights of fame,
Be graceful, talented and herald acclaim!

Not one that November did foresee
This child would become enchanting, Vivien Leigh!*

---

* Vivien Leigh was born in Darjeeling, India, November 5, 1913, Guy Fawkes night.

Vivien

Quivering patterns of another tomorrow fade away,
But my love for you stays eternal,
Ethereal angel from another time.
The bewitching charm behind the mesh,
perfection veiled and promising,
Then the tinkle of the Chinese lantern
when she smiles ... illuminating my life.

Enchantress

A sorceress who caste her spell
With dancing eyes like whirlpools of aquamarine!

In Her Words

She was a celestial Scorpion
Who ate herself up and burnt herself out.

She swayed between happiness and misery
Crying easily, loving devotedly.

She was part prude, part non-conformist,
She said what she thought and didn't dissemble.

Star Light

This is she, who graced the stage,
Held our attention in awe.
This is she, who took our breath away
In all that she played.
This is she, who vowed us with her mythical beauty,
Floated instead of walking,
Shrouded in star light.

Comet

She was more than a shining star,
Alike to Halley's comet;
Once in a lifetime
And like a comet
Her radiant energy was suddenly quenched.

Reminiscence*

An old man sits
Watching wistfully,
Love that the heart shall miss
Screen flickers silver imagery.

He'd forgotten her lyrical voice,
How she'd kissed him through two centuries;
In darkness here rejoice,
Clouded, but now alive sweet memories.

Tears prick the back of his eyes,
They must have lost the eternal ring,
In silence and regret he cries
"This, this was love. This was the real thing."

---

* *In 1986, a visitor to Laurence Olivier's home witnessed him watching a Vivien Leigh film in tears. Olivier had sat crying saying, "This, this was love. This was the real thing." Olivier by Anthony Holden, pg. 112. They had divorced in 1960 after nearly twenty-four years together. Vivien passed away in 1967, Olivier in 1989.*

The Picture

Morning rays filter through,
Creating mystical patterns—
A frame to keep you recognised.

Perfect Celtic face,
Exquisite almond eyes,
Flower-like beauty
That heaven's angles cannot deny—
Delicate like the first dew on a rose petal

A paradox:
Determined steely reserve,
Diamond reconnaissance,
Watch over me as I rise—
Inspire my day.

Butterfly

Part mythical creature, part Southern belle!

She came looking for the streetcar,
This butterfly engulfed in chiffon dreams,
She was trying to fix her wounded wings.

The pastel paper lanterns
And pink cottage roses,
Surrounded her recovery.

She wanted magic, not reality,
Trying to survive against brutality
And those who pulled at her wings.

Living in her perfume castle,
Dressed in peach lace and pearls,
Depending forever on the kindness of strangers.

The Actress

Patterns of light and shadow
Waltz on the screen
Projections convey multi-layered perceptions.

She puts on another a mask,
But some have stuck
Another illusion.

Remnants of Scarlett remain,
And we who burn incense at her altar
Cannot see her.

And she wants magic, she cried,
Yes, yes, MAGIC!

Lady Macbeth

Oh, menacing night,
Not revealed in the light,
Possessed with guilt and ghosts
Comes my beautiful viper
From beneath her flower.

Seductive in her moves,
Intent in her gaze,
Slithering to her husband's glory,
Alluring in her insistence.

But alas, the story goes,
When the King's deed was done,
Could not let herself rest:
Out, damn spot!
Could not endure her tortured mind.

Beguiling was she in her madness,
Hypnotic in her starring trance,
Mythic was her performance,
Transcendent and ethereal;
Stunning and unforgettable,*
All hail her, Lady Macbeth!

---

* *In 1955 Vivien played Lady Macbeth in Laurence Olivier's Macbeth. Her performance was not well received. Critics felt her too delicate and not good enough beside Olivier. This caused her much distress and even contributed to a breakdown. What's disappointing is that after her death, most did a complete turnaround on their assessment. Her biggest critique, Kenneth Tynan, admitted it was the worst misjudgment of his career. Olivier, who would be acclaimed as the best actor of his generation, in his book On Acting classed her as the best Lady Macbeth that he had ever seen.*

Moonlight*

She walks in the moonlight,
The beautiful and melancholy moonlight,
Like a dream in a Venetian masquerade,
Not believing her song was true;
Floating in a magical vista
Encircled by sadness, dancing in ruins.

She walks in the moonlight,
The beautiful and melancholy moonlight,
Through his evergreen folly,
Awaiting the call that never came;
Like a young boy waltzing through
The stream, sobbing its desolate tune.

---

* *Vivien Leigh loved to walk in nature. Unable to sleep, she would walk through the woods at Tickerage and fields around Notley. Peter Finch, remembering her after her death, in an interview, saw her as a young boy walking through Ceylon's ruins and in the wind near Notley. Hugo Vickers, Vivien Leigh, pg. 357.*

She walks in the moonlight,
The beautiful and melancholy moonlight,
Through whimsical, dew-scattered meadows
Covered in tangled reflections;
Mellowed nightmares by lunar beams
Her heartache and confusion, somehow endurable.

Poetic Tragedy

Dresden shepherdess lies in bed,
Hair pulled up revealing swan neck;
She smiles, enticing her watcher,
But somewhere deep inside
She succumbs to her poetic tragedy.

Tickerage Lake*

In this pond of enchantment lies
Tickerage winds, blowing the melody of her heartbreak;
Leaves rustling and echoing her sweet laughter,
Bluebells yonder woods swaying like her slender hips,
And she sleeps at long last with
Water lilies as her crown.

---

* *Tickerage Mill was the last home of Vivien Leigh. Located in Uckfield, near the village of Blackboys, the mill is decorated by a tranquil lake, where her ashes were scattered in 1967.*

CHILDREN

Pencil sketch of Vivien Leigh at six months with her mother, Gertrude Hartley, 1914, India. Photo included in the Early Life album belonging to Vivien Leigh. Acquired by Vivien Leigh Circle and donated to Victoria and Albert Museum.

This, My Son*

"'Sleep now,' they said, 'and rest the whole night through,'
And left me till the dawn.
How could I sleep, my very little one?
When all my thoughts were crying out to you."
Joan Kinmont

---

* *Part of poem: This, My Son, was written by Australian writer, Joan Kinmont, in 1943. It sold over 100,000 copies and was reprinted in 1945 with a preface by Australian Prime Minister, John Curtain. The author is lucky to own the copy she presented to Vivien Leigh and Laurence Olivier during their 1948, Old Vic Tour of Australia and New Zealand.*

Blessed

When they graced my womb,
I was given my life's meaning;
And the gods – they were dancing.

Old Souls

Both my children had old-soul eyes,
So said the nurses who took them.
Wonder-filled, they both came

Eyes wide open,

Taking in as much as they could,
Looking like they had known the world before;
Eager to teach me all they knew.

Daughter

You are a fierce spirit
Embodied with fire in your soul,
Molded by a miracle of the universe,
A masterpiece evolved through time;
Bathed from stardust,
Every particle precious,
Unique, like the rarest diamond,
To bring love on the marble planet
And to create HER story.

You are more than my child!

Caring One

I still remember that day, my son,
When, like a big boy you packed your bag—
First day of kinder, it will be fun.

There were no nerves or fears,
My heart overflowed with pride,
But my eyes pricked with tears.

This, my first day without you near,
And you, such a little child,
Revealed your caring nature there.

For down the path you went,
Holding tightly onto grandpa's hand—
You walked ahead with intent.

Then, like a sparrow to his mother,
You turned and ran back into my arms
And cried, "Will you be OK without me?"

Peaceful One

My little Bali Rani came as a surprise,
All wrapped up in beautiful serenity;
Not a night did I lose sleep.

A peaceful child with always smiles,
Content to watch with eyes of wonder;
Never to cry and cause worry.

What did I do to deserve such a rose?
Unexpected, and surely a gift;
To become the heiress of my heart.

Night Time

Whenever you fear the dark
And your small heart beats too fast,
Look up into the night sky;
Gaze with your soulful eyes upon the stars
With your innocent untrampled wonder—
For it's only at night, sweetheart
We can see the wonder of our heaven.

Dear Christina,
Wherever your earth voyage takes you,
Never be afraid of the dark.

Kittoo

Kittoo, my Little Bali Rani!
Do you love me – because
I love you more,
Don't you see?

Kittoo, my Little Bali Rani!
I love you to the moon and back, moon and back;
I'll love you more than that!
Don't you see?

Kittoo, my Little Bali Rani!
I love you to the stars, comets – to infinity;
No one else will love you like that,
Don't you see?

Kittoo, my Little Bali Rani!
My one and only.

Star Gazing

Look up, dear heart,
Whenever you are lonely;
See where darkness meets a spray of spangled lights?
Know there is one that shines just for you.

Look up, dear heart,
Whenever you are lost;
See the star of the north shining bright?
Know that its compass will bring you home.

Enlightened

"They came through you, not from you," said the prophet,
So, our prayer for children:
We stand still as the bow,
And on your flight, find the story already written;
It is in the glorious morning sky,
In that moment within when we let go.

Remember your sweet innocence,
See the glistening first dew,
Embrace the wonder,
Smell the lilacs too:
Witness the miracle
And feel the love.

Before you forget who you are,
Be not what they want:
Be true, son and daughter,
Then and ONLY then you are YOU.

LOVE

Vivien Leigh and Laurence Olivier

* Pencil sketch of Vivien Leigh and Laurence Olivier, Life cover, 1951, Philippe Halsman.

Unending Love

"I seem to have loved you in numberless forms,
numberless times ...
In life after life, in age after age, forever.
My spellbound heart has made and remade
the necklace of songs,
That you take as a gift, wear round your neck
in your many forms,
In life after life, in age after age, forever."
RABINDRANATH TAGORE

* Rabindranath Tagore was a Bengali poet, novelist and painter, considered the greatest writer of Indian literature. He was the first non-European to be awarded the Nobel Prize for Literature in 1913 for his book of verse, Gitanjali (Song Offerings). Quote, first verse of poem, 'Unending Love': Gitanjali.

Love Letters[*]

These words they sent across the oceans,
They sailed to an orchestra of sealed memories,
Recording all of their nostalgic yesterdays.

These words they sent across the oceans,
Testaments to their love undenied,
Proclamations of unquestioned devotion.

These words they sent across the oceans,
Terrified of revealing their clandestine love,
Their heart's blood unable to live apart.

---

[*] *The Victoria & Albert Museum in London houses 200 plus letters from the Vivien Leigh Estate, and the British Library houses the Laurence Olivier Archive. Leigh and Olivier's letters to each other reveal the depth of their legendary love. Some unashamedly show how passionate, illicit and erotic it was at the start. Others show Olivier's concern for Leigh's health and career. Both write of their anguish at being apart. After their divorce the correspondence still continued, some at times grieving their lost love.*

These words they sent across the oceans,
Lustful tender and enchanting,
Enquiring endlessly of her wellness.

These words they sent across the oceans,
Fighting to keep heartache at bay,
Pleading for their love to stay.

These words they sent across the oceans,
Nightmares of their lost happiness,
Praying their sadness softly blows away.

These words they sent across the oceans,
Now safe in treasured archives,
Waiting to be awakened by a Yours Sincerely.

"Whenever you think of me my Larry-boy
you will know I am with you.
Your adoring Vivling"*

"You are in my thoughts and weighing so heavily
in my heart all the time.
I am only existing until I see you again ...
Larry"†

---

* Excerpt 1. Leigh from Italy to Oliver at Notley Abbey, 1956. The Laurence Olivier Archive, The British Museum.
† Excerpt 2. Olivier to Leigh date unknown –1938/39? The Vivien Leigh Archive, Victoria and Albert Museum.

> "Whatever happens let us be friends my dearest one ... I shall love you all my life with a tenderness and respect that is all embracing ... My love dear dear Heart
> Vivling"*

---

* Excerpt 3. Leigh to Olivier, June 20th, 1960, The Laurence Olivier Archive, The British Museum.

Spilled Ink[*]

Ink bleeds their truth,
Each mind's eye melted into words,
Their souls laid bare on periwinkle,
Only worthy of one another.

---

[*] *Vivien Leigh's personalised Smythson stationary was a very distinctive colour – periwinkle.*

Penship

This pen spills ink,
Bleeding pieces of you in each word it forms.

Embrace

Let us descend into each other's eyes,
Our breaths mold to synchronicity,
Heartbeats rise to the same rhythm.

Let us see a caravan of dreams pass
Through our dilated ebony pools,
To evanesce into each other's arms.

Poisonous Lust

You are the poison
I look forward to devouring
To bring life to me.

You are the venom
I inject into my veins
To push my blood faster.

You are the fatal perfume
I inhale to intoxicate
To help me see not reason.

You, you, you,
I will die helplessly
On the eroticism of your cashmere.

Seduction

Seduce me with the words you whispered in my ear,
The portrait you paint of my flight,
Come to me in my dreams of Neverland
When I can only think of you in the darkness of my aloneness.

Seduce me with the pictures you help me imagine,
The scent in a field of wild roses,
Come to me in baby's breath,
When the pain of past losses shatters my beating heart.

Seduce me with visions of our minds entwining,
The kiss to take my life's meaning,
Come to me in the seconds before my last blink,
When the last image will be of your saving grace.

Seduce me with your intelligent caress,
The understanding of my mind's struggle,
Come to me when I'm trying to inspire,
When all that's needed is self-belief and passion.

Seduce me with images of yesterday's nostalgia,
The message that awakens my sleeping soul,
Come to me as the words to my story are lost
When you have ripped apart my logic.

Seduce me again with past pleasures,
The story of their great romance,
Come to me in the words they exchanged, now dusty archives,
When through their lives we make our own travels.

Seduce me with one last imaginary kiss,
The longing glance I dream you'll give,
Come to me with the flowers you might've picked
When finally, the diary is filled and overflowing with our love.

Darlings of Gods

A desire like a thousand windswept storms,
They chased passion like chasing its rain,
Clinging to a frivolous, yet all-consuming embrace,
Clearing to a blossoming day canopied by a mythical rainbow:
To be surpassed by the blinding light of tomorrow
And eclipsed by the gloom of a jealous, ominous cloud,
Leaving their sketch on love's legendary landscape
For mortals to dream of
And that was their love.

The Sea and the Moon

She was his moon,
He was her sea.

She made him rise—
And he adored her magnificence.

Arabian Night

Warm gust of Arabian winds,
Come, bring me my lover,
Carry him on a palanquin of dazzling dragon flies.

Sweet Indian summer night,
Caress the moon as she fixes her gaze
On my love, as he descends into my awaiting arms.

Mystical and erotic jasmine flower,
Intoxicate me and my love
So, we entwine in an ecstatic trance.

Prisoner

Come steal me away
And imprison me in the most sacred
Chamber of your heart
Where I will succumb to the rhythm of your love.

Destiny

Lovers destined for each other,
Placed from the palm of Aphrodite,
Have no concern for social graces,
Nor the wisdom of years,
When they finally meet.
They will confront their destiny,
And the moons they shall collide.

Fate

Maybe one day, My Darling,
people will read our love story
and yearn for a moment like ours.

Maybe one day, My Dearest,
They will feel the conjuring
Of our stars colliding.

Maybe one day, My Sweetheart,
Lovers will identify the ordinance
When we confronted our destiny.

Desirious Sea

Let me summon these winds to carry my forbidden words to you over the Caspian Sea ...
I love you.

From Here to Eternity

The orchestra of the sea
welcomed the lovers' naked feet
As its froth covered them in ecstasy.

Bodies consumed with passion
Swim out to a world without end.

Moments

This moment, this precious moment ...
When true love shines through your gorgeous eyes;
I know for certain you're mine.
When the past does not enter the equation
And I see clearly life's meaning.
When the wounds we inflicted suddenly heal,
And we are without the stain of betrayal.
When in our innocence all was perfect—

Quick, catch it before it vanishes ...

Red Wine Memories

Red wine, rain me a glass of memories,
Spill all over my breaking heart,
Red wine, kiss my thirsty lips,
Make me speak my heart's poetry,
Until the memories of him arrive.

Summer Love

As the twilight sky gets lacquered in a scarlet glow
And the lunar moon appears for her final ovation,
I sit quietly with memories, sweet beau!

Wishing to remember that summer day so clearly now!

Before sunrise, we ran to the secret cove,
Dancing on soft sand with entangled hands,
Into crashing waves of Apollo Bay, we dove.

Oh, I remember that summer day so clearly now!

You wrapped the towel, embracing me,
My naked shoulder betrothed a tender kiss,
As the new day dawned, Australian gulls flew free.

Yes, I remember that summer day so clearly now!

The fish and chips at the corner store
Made salty lips that you possessed,
Drunk on youthful love, uncommitted bliss we wore.

Be still, I remember that summer day so clearly now!

As the twilight sky gets lacquered in a scarlet glow
And the lunar moon takes her final ovation
Twelve Apostles cliffs beckoned us so!

Oh, I remember that summer day so clearly now!

The evening breeze tousled your golden hair,
You turned and said, "I love you" hopeful in your eyes,
I was speechless for a second, I swear.

Stay, for I remember that summer day so clearly now!

If I had that moment again
I'd say it back …

Oh, I remember that summer day so clearly now!

Burnt

Did we run into a burning house
To save something once loved?
Did we give it all a second chance?
Passions once loved, saved,
But here we are trapped,
Engulfed by the smoke of torture,
Lost in our madness,
Waiting to be saved ourselves.

Flame

Deep within me there is a lake
Where eternal hope floats,
And in my memories the scent of the love I lost.

Scars

My sweet, tell me your story,
Show me your wounds,
Read aloud to me each chapter
Including the ending.
Reveal to me the beauty you hide,
The love you're afraid to give,
Uncover to me your cuts
And then I'll still love **you,**
And you'll see love through love's eyes.

Remembrance

We may not get marked in history,
Nor engraved in stone,
Nor sung about;
But here in a poem,
A sentence,
In between a stanza, a page, a word
and a breath,
Maybe someone might remember us.

Yours

Ever mine,
Take me on a journey,
To lead me back to you.
Every turn,
Wistful in search,
Show me my fate,
Ever thine.

Enchanted Love

As twilight's curtain falls,
We laid down our heads
On summer's sweet grass,
Humbled by God's collection of stars above.

On this precious peak,
Rocky castle that holds the land,
Imposing summit swallows our pride.

Engulfed by Norsca air,
We lie loved till morning.

And then—
Awe at the serenading of dawn!

Photograph of Vivien Leigh and Laurence Olivier, 1948, Australia, exact date and location unknown, from an album comprising of personal snap shots from the Old Vic tour of Australia and New Zealand. The author acquired this album from the Sotheby's Vivien Leigh Estate auction in 2017.

www.ingramcontent.com/pod-product-compliance
Lightning Source LLC
Chambersburg PA
CBHW021113080526
44587CB00010B/504